The Ethereal Mansion

By Dorian Grey

Table of Contents

I extent my appreciation to Zak Albano
for creating my book cover.

Welcome

The ethereal mansion looms under the dusky sky
Thunder crashes, lightning flashes
Through the dull colors of the enlightened
Entering the mansion
Your Senses roam
Like vultures in the desert heat
Closed eyes
Opened mind
Receiving hands
Grounded feet
Come on in, pace about, stand in one place, kneel on the carpet or
sit in a chair
How ever you wish to posture yourself, just remember , to be silent,
listen and be open to all that haunts this mansion

Do not be afraid for all that lurks in these halls and walls, for they
are not here to harm but to help
Come, move with the shadows
Come, move through the visions
Open the doors of perception
Embrace the Ethereal Mansion

This is all that is

Sitting upon a rooftop

Sitting with the birds, perched and waiting for the wind to call us
forwards, onwards to the cloud covered kaleidoscope

In those wings, in these pattering hearts

This is spring, this is the fresh start

A new part from your feet that are in concrete of the lock step with
all the rest

Look kitten you can fly like a magpie

I saw you sitting on the mountaintop

Perched on the precipice, sitting under the full moon night

Your silhouette shimmering with the nectar of the night

Running down the mountain side, the milk and honey, changed
every nook and cranny every rock and pore began to awake and
move

For it is no longer just Mohammed that can move mountains

As the mountain awoke and moved in that same full moon night

I saw you dancing with a great fire, the eternal fire, void less and on
top of the mountain

Inside a giant sphere of silhouettes lingering in mystery

As I gazed on, in silent contemplation
I learned to stand at the foot of the mountain, embracing the eternal
fire and dancing with the one who can move mountains

Yet I don't not ask any questions
For I need not know any answers

For in this night surrounding the ether
In the great fire, the eternal fire
Is A sphinx without a secret

This is all that is
This is all that needs to be
This is all you miss when you look to the future and try and
remember the past
Moving mountains is the here and now
This is all that is

The Alphabet in Alliterations appear Above the Alpha

The beauty blasts and blows at beaches and blisters the Bravo

The Cantaloupe, the Cranberries, canter with Colonels and Charlie

The dance of dregs drench the design of Delta

The elephant erases the errands of electric ether with Echo

The front foot forgoes the foreshadowing of the Foxtrot

The Giraffe's gazing while grazing is like guessing when playing Golf

The healing and the helium help humans reach a higher Hotel

The inside of insects intersects the inner circle of India

The jester will jest about, as the jaguar jeers at Juliet

The Kangaroo kicks the keeper of Kilo

The laying and lounging of lady's look's like a Lima

The Moment the moor moved, the minstrel messed with Mike

The Newtonian notion of knowing needs November

The opal was the open obsession of Wilde's Oscar

The parrot will pardon the present in presence of Papa

The quiet quest is quaking the quagmire of Quebec

The racoon rants at the rabbit in riots lead by Romeo

The sunrises surmise surrounds the scene in Sierra

The 2 toed tap dancer taps and twirls the Tango

The urchin uses the umbrella as a Uniform

The viceroy ventures in vices and forgets about virtues Victory

The wino whistles and wishes for Whiskey

The extreme expressive use of exuberance will explain the X-rays

The yellow yeast yields yelling from Yankees

The zebra zigs and zags on the zones of Zulu

Writing Nothing

I am writing, I am writing about nothing, for nothing is profound,
nothing is exactly the perfect notion, to sit, embrace and write
The pen becomes everything, is everywhere, is the reason I write
Its not for knowledge, that I write
I write to feel the soft, friction of pen on paper, like the warm body,
under the kool of sheets
The warm sun, among the coldest of winters
The coursing of blood through the darkest of hearts
I write to bring fourth, life, from the shadows, from the death
I write to resurrect the 2nd coming
I write to hammer a nail in the lid of the coffin or maybe to pry open
that same coffin lid
And have the books move about in a state of pestilence
I write for nothing in particular, for that is everything, that everything
turns the nothing then stirs the truth in life
Into the void, I write to hang every word into the void, to sail with
every written letter, with every written syllable, for every written
word is a gate opening into the void of nothing
The life blood of everything

I am writing about nothing, in black and blue
I am writing, are you confused?
Nothing, is everything
Nothing is where you will be

And nothing is from where you came to be

Nothingness is the game

That's why I am writing

Its my muse…..bishop to Queen 4

Nothing

The taste of nothing is so sweet

The smell of nothing is so scintillating

The touch of nothing is pure bliss

The seeing of nothing is moving

The pressure of nothing is bold and encompassing

The essence of nothing is the ethereal dripping

I am writing about nothing, nothing, nothing

Come join me, writing, floating into the the abyss of true life relieved

This is nothing, I am writing about all this, for just holding onto the pen and dragging it across the paper is nothing, this is nothing, this nothing is everything

Your move… Pawn to King 7

Check mate

Crawl Onwards

I see you Crawling, clawing, climbing and crumbling into the origins
of the original oceans, with blue brilliant, blistering balls of string,
straining to secure you into safety and survival of the systems that
have helped in heeding your head into slavery

this is the same steeple that we find skeletons sprawled across the

open atmosphere of abstract arrays

like zebra skins

the zig zag wanderers roam in rants and riots

of "this is safe as milk"

now Captain Beef Heart is singing to the roots of recited rights of
rage and rhetoric

its is exactly esoteric to stare and speak into the open chasm of
chaos and find calamity clinging to the crippled skeletons

as the skulls are dangling on the ceiling fan In 4/4 time

we try to open the doors of perception

we try and steer up the stairs to reach the right-handed star

its the same scene and sense on 7th and 9th street, that we find
the wizards and witches wading in the water

swimming, stammering, stumbling into the origins of octagonal
objects of Love, Lust and Livelihood

Listen and leap into the abyss of alabaster Air

Apparently, applying apples to apartment, will leave a linger scent
of wonderful nectar

right now nihilism was never such a waste of kneeling

so, keep crawling, clawing, climbing and crumbling into the origins
of the absurd rituals

as the jesters and jugglers jest about jaguars in perfect pictures,
framed of famous fumes and vintage furs

Catch for us the foxes that frolic in the farmyards

as lepers leap in Lily-dale an

and leprechauns lick lilacs in lakes

to rewrite the ways of societies, these societies are encased in cities that care for creating caricatures of their VIPs and MVP's in the same picture frames of the famous forums and vintage furs

forever skeletons will dance in darkness and dresses to decree

that we should stop creeping, crawling, clawing, climbing and crumbling not the origins of light and loathsome levels of ritual rites

so onward to the open doors

run down the carpet's hallways and trip on the tactical knowledge that is trying to keep you thinking, thinking and studying and caring about where and why and when you make your bed

lay down into the origins of our ancestors

let go of what is being built in the attic

and become the addict of being apart of the ascended homo sapience

Playful Pride

Pizza, Pizza, Pizza pies

Pie is a present of 3.14 with parts of purpose

Filling pangs of pain, which become poetry with practice

Puzzles and precise preaching lead to plateaus and precipices for the price of prestigious postures

The pistol is purple

The pen is pink

The pointing is prying open the problems with the popular people

Please, print on the pages of papers and propose to the pedals of pansies and paragraphs that are in possession of pleasure to the polite pressures of pressing power into a pocketful of pennies

Pamphlets of peace

Persons of pets

The pantheon is full of pictures and paintings

Panthers prowl and perch in the past and ponce in the present to find proper prey

Pray for the princess and the pea as they look for the prince of the pauper

Prancing with puppets in the photo lab of privilege

Prepare the puppies and preoccupy the papayas

The Birth of Tragedy

I do believe is something higher then this but I don't know how to fly

so take me down, lay me down into the sky

and begin to transmigrate into the 3rd eye

Walk down that hall ways and open the doors of perception to find
the universe sitting in infamy and infinitely in cased in dreams

you'll find Soren Kierkegaard and Fredrick Nietzsche sipping coffee
in utter wondering of experience

as Aldous Huxley is Witting about A Brace New World and show us
how society will be enshrined to this

they will cry for white washed tombs and forget the beauty of their
mothers wombs

As they devise the will to beat the world of Sisyphus and the life of
struggle

They fight against the role of rolling the boulder up the mountain to
have it all crash back down

Fighting against the very essence of nature, never finding peace

never to realize that we are born into the birth of tragedy

They are the example of plastic thinking

We must forget our fetters and let the universe sink in

forget that we are the artist

and become the work of art

Dance, because we have forgotten how to walk, how to talk, how to
listen and to think

Dance because we have procured wings and can fly to a god like
enchantment
an enchantment not of Icarus but of Dionysus
not of death but of transmigration
not of prideful thinking but of transcend living

Dying spectre

He seemed like a spirit of the sea
A shaman to the conjuring of existential beings
As he walked before me, into the other side, illuminating and glowing
A form cast in the lock step with the sea
It shall all be seen
Revealing what lies beyond the veil

Seemingly rare, naked and bare
Esoteric, spontaneous, and not for all eyes to share

The snow, like the soul, sustained under white light, white heat
And lets the power of summer rest in the winter, far below
Like the snow, he walks in a around the dead, sleeping trees
Swaying in the ocean's depths
20,000 leagues under the sea

Professor Aronnax speaks, we are to close to Hades
Captain Nemo replies, we are still to close to Heaven

Soon all this wont matter, anti matter
Humans dismal canter, the surfaces banter
As we all fall to the wake of the seas
White light, white heat
For we are all dying spectres dancing 20,000 leagues under the sea

Open

Open the occult

Be obliged to observe the oppression

Over and over the observations are over the oven

Occupy the oceans

As octopi and orange organisms oscillate on the oval in octaves

Obsidian, opals, and opera

Open the oysters for obstacles and objects as they obey the others, who opened the other side of the outer orbits and oddities with odes form the oracles?

Listen for the ocarina

For the ozone is obedient to old Ben or maybe the mean old Obe one konbi?

Suppose So

People say they know so
but People don't know, they only suppose so
they try and live like royalty but have attitudes that fall so low
and find reality so slow
as they figure that they must know so
But OH No, Darwin has showed so, that we reap what we sow
we breath what we blow
we sink far below, what we suppose so
we now dig our graves with a flat hoe
and think we are pro
but we do not know so
we assume so
and support that it all must be so, of what we know so
yet our reactions to change is so slow and beauty has died in a
distracted, disgusting, horrific show
we have lost touch with what we know so
we have let the rich and blind lead the show bringing the "Art of
lying" far below, what Oscar Wilde try to show in his written show
so forget what we know so, let go of what we suppose so
let go of all the false control and rise above the Ego that lies below
for rising about this ego
Is the name of the game and show
remember you don't actually know so, and what you suppose so is
only learned from reading what people thought was so
so let go of that ego
and keep learning, unlearning all that you suppose so and think you
know so

Yesterday

Yesterday yearns for the yes and for you to yawn towards the yogurts
yokes

You'll find yoga with the youth of yester-years yelling and yodeling to the
yellow yachtsmen

They yammer to the Yankees and yonder to the yule logs

You are use to yours and yours to use and abuse yesterday

Yesterday you will yield the yellow fever and watch the yakking yak talk

back

You can be your own worst enemy in every year book and yellow pages

Separatist

As a separatist, I feel the unity in the cause of being capable to influence the masses

To bond together in the cause of being a new revolution to unify

A massive part of influence is community

Making a island into a continent

They might have their guns but we have the numbers

This is the inertia to the separatists cause

Sitting during a separatists silent sermon

Standing hand in hand for a peaceful demonstration

Supporting a movement of "not to be labeled like the rest"

as the current system has let so many of our brothers and sisters, slide, fizzle and disappear through the cracks

As that system has let the best minds of our generation be destroyed by madness and pornography

It is now our time to be separatists and stand up for Love, Peace and Understanding

As they have labeled us Separatists

So separatist we shall be, uniting the masses and standing up for our future

Dancing

The dukes of Denmark drink and drank deadwood while dealing dismal damage to the drains of the darkness

2 dancing duchess, dipped deeply into the decades of days as they began to dream of diving into deliriums daze

We shall dance through deaths valley

As the doors will decide to drive us into depths of doom as it all turns upside down

We watch the dance of demigods and deities as they deactivate the decree

Which delayed David from being deprived form Delilah

Dead trees dig dead roots into dark dirt

Darling, did you know that disco deserves deaf digits?

Did you know that disc jockeys use dexterity to decode dancing in dub step?

A desert, In searching

I don't know where I'm going, I don't know where I'm heading

So I took the dagger from my back

Framed it, hung it on my wall

In remembrance to never look back

In remembrance of our catastrophe fall

From embracing each other as lovers, to becoming the silhouettes of
infinite strangers

Moving along a path laden with dead roses, dying lotus leaves

As helpless we must be wandering a desert in searching for something that
can never be

I don't know where I'm heading, I don't know where I'm going

But I feel the warm, tender sun on my back

I gaze upon it, I commit it to memory

In vivid perceptions of looking forward, in conception of grace and danc-

ing onwards

Form the distance of complete strangers, moving into the presence of pure
lovers

Journeying along a path enhanced by grace and understanding, living in
laughter

As helpful we must be wandering a desert in search of something we can
always be

Playful thoughts

The arithmetic of language

Conceiving shapes, numbers and other properties distinct and absent of our 6 senses

I think, Therefore I am

where does thought bury its stem?

Is it in all of us or just them?

Jump into the void-less, Shapeless entity

That has been and will forever be

Moving in the eternal return

The playful language

Metaphysical yearning to dance with knowledge

From one thought to the next

Passed down by

Schiller to Dewey

Rousseau to Hobbs

Machiavelli to Nietzsche

The minds that thought and flexed

The Xylophonist

The xerox explains, how the xylophonist is existing in xanex
Also how does the xylophonist plays the xylophone while reading x-rays
Now the xyloid brings fourth extreme excitement

The Apartment

There's a cat, there's a chair

Sitting in a love seat next to us

In a small, yet medium, feeling flat with broken, pined up luxurious colors
bleeding down the walls

No blemishes, no cracks

Just love and snacks

In this apartment

Dust

A Pessimist is a form of determination

Wrapping itself around the absurdity that we all have control, under
blissful situation of living

Breathing, surviving in this mad hatter hour glass

As it shatters into the chaos, that is life,

positioned and meticulous, the dust is gathering

On the march hares tea set

A life of meaning

Duality… will bring it into shape

Polarity… will show you the hook and bate

Existential… will tear the rope asunder

Meat-physical… will bare realities under

A life of conscience surrendering will birth a life of profound finding

Once we learn that freedom is dying and oneself must be forgotten and left
in the light… ever blinding

Contradiction… a place of mud and grime, nothing clear

Distraction… A slight of hand, staring at the mirror

Peaceful action… A hand shake in a distressed event

Unified Faction… A place of understanding, a true ascent

A life of transcendent beckoning will open a portal to realities of
reckoning once we truly love and stop heckling

Oneself must be released from the darkness… ever blinding

Quarters

Q-tips, Quarries, Quarrels are quietly asking questions that quack

Quake the quagmires quadrant

Be queer

Quest for the quail and quantum queens will qualify for the quick-slivers, quicksand

Quarantine queues the quick witted quid pro qou

don't quit the quiz but keep quoting loves quirky quintessential quotas

Exit, enter

Everyone is acting out of pride
Yet, we do not exist
We just float inside the morning mist
Its all vapour, we are all vapour
A spectre of the ghost in the midst of a locked closet with no clothes
Its on fire from the inside yet the matches are in the next room
What actually exists?
Exit through the enter and fall into the beauty of non- existence, abyss

Paid

Everything has been paid
The sensation, the burden of being
Seeing how we are well taken care of
Its time to feel heavenly blessed and loss this earths happiness
Let us bond together and build a village of sorts
Everything is paid for

Lyrical styles

A style. Lyrical, tempo-ed, measured and instituted

To relay nothing

To the eye of the witness

To the eye of the witness, the rhythm is planned with purpose, to demonstrate a reverb into the synopsis of the syndrome

Across the room and the walls to the rhymed time with stylistic, lyrics on the tempo-ed measured intersected pages

A stylish, lyrical, tempo-ed measured inter-sectioned

Eye

To relay nothing to the passers by

To the eyes of the passers by, this is rhythm-ed and planned without purpose

Yet demonstrates, the reverb into the synopsis of the systems that carry across the room, the halls, the walls, the streets, in its rhymed time

With the stylistic lyrics of the first tempo-ed, measured pages that are instituted

Cocooned

In cased in a cocoon in the ceiling of the curling cells

Cyclones in cylinders cascade the cavalcade of chaos

And create the calm cartoons that help in charity and find clarity

As we enjoy the crumbs of crumble cake

Cough after cigarettes and coffee while we build the house of cards from
cardboard and confetti

Cepherus is sitting and citing cancers crazy cure

As cannery's cry for the catalyst to creeps into the children's creation of
characters passing at the crossroad

Collect the crimson connections and find the carbon copies of cynical

Casanova

As cats and cougar are certain they can claw through the clairvoyants

casket

Transportation

I enjoy taking the bus
The interconnection is unfathomable
To the essence of community

The embodiment of masses
They all swipe passes
The riders are cast in many forms
Passing and moving in human conversations

While sitting in a row of uncomfortable seats
Next to a stranger
Friends and persons living in clear proximity of one another

The Bus is a public servitude to ensure
We can always smile at each-other

Unconscious

Open the wound

Find that the blood flows without conscience thought

Soulfully flowing past and through all the entities that are all the parts that
make up the body

Open the body

Find the many pulsing muscles, pumping in unity without conscience
thought

Soulfully electrifying and passing though the stems of connections,
underneath the flesh

Close your eyes

Close your mind

Relax and feel the constant flow into the streams and stems without any
conscience thought

Eating

The eating of epidemiology edifies and eradicates the esoteric ears

Whiling eating everything else, has the effect of electric elastic epitaph

Erase the errands of eloping elevations

The elections on earth are elected by earth worms and eclipse earthquakes
each time we try to educate each-other on the egocentric elixirs

While everlasting escalators are escaping through eating eerie emeralds of
encouraging the emergencies on endless end-papers

Enjoy the eating of the enigmas energy

Envelope the enlightened and extol of eating for eternity

There is an extra existence in the ethos and ethereal extinction that will
erupt the everlasting eyes of everything, everywhere

As it all expands in the experience

Be Here

The adoration of the old
Brings
The inspiration to the new
Watch your mind
You must understand the past to expand the future
Watch your mind
Think during all situations
Listen to what people are saying
Be coherent of your ears
If its truly a fault, listen for the change
If its truly false, let it just flow on by
Watch your mind
React with compassion towards your fellow humans

The Desert

There's something kool about the desert

The desolation, the peace, the vast void in which you can never fully
traverse

The open, the dust, the life,

A place to get lost in dreams

As they shift away through the ever moving grains of sand

Its all bat country and manta rays

Climbing down the air raids

a great play to experience the fine line of life and death

And realities pure existence

We are

We smoke. We choke. We always poke the bigger bloke. And he votes. In fisticuffs

His thumps. His Bumps. We end up in a slump.

What a fight. As we choke on smoke from the bloke we poked. That bloke Stands above us.

Plus were spitting puss. Blood covered by crud. So we play dead in the soiled mud. Soaked in suds.

We smoke. We drink. We fornicate. We gamble. We ramble. We blink. We are humans. We are flawed. We see the Gods and applaud.

We are fragile. We enjoy vices. We forget virtues. We stand and curse you.

We are ritualistic. We are powerfully picturesque . We are futuristic. We are forgotten rhetoric

We are failing forward. We are Fainting for fortified failures.

We are. ………. We are……….. We are

Notions

The notions of knowing is noted in a note book

There isn't any news that's new, that isn't nearly nonsense

With noisy neighbors their natter is nihilistic and they narrowly need the
Nile

Never negate nothing, for the knowing of knowledge is nothing

Never the less learn the inertia of the necktie remedy and notice the
nations napalm

In the northern nooks

The newts will follow newtons notions of neptunium neutrons

We must nullify, we must nurture, we must nudge nature so that none will

die kneeling

But we must notice the knocking of the nine inch nails

In the neck of the nectar

With the negative negotiations it will be normal in the nomads of nostalgia

Cannot to Can To

you cannot write, if you cannot read
You cannot eat, if you cannot chew
You cannot play, if you cannot sleep
You cannot walk, if you cannot stand
You cannot be wise, if you cannot listen
You cannot dance, if you cannot crawl
The cannot are full of cans,
in reverence we find love
In surrender we find peace
In death we find penitence
In all the cannot's with can find the can To's
Switch, shift, skew your visions of conceptions and find all the can to's
For all is possible when you change your perspectives

Words and words

Spell the spell. Split the spill. Dream the dream. beam towards the beam. Try the tire. Tear the tear. Spear the spare. Sport the sport. Spot the spot. Save the safe. Signal the sign. Sign for the signal. Die for death. Death is dead. Dead is deaf. Defeat the decaf. Drink the drank. Drank the. Drunk. Drunk the drink.

KEEP

Keep the mind racing. Keep the eyes pacing. Keep the feet tapping. Keep the fingers rapping. Keep the pen writing. Keep the paper fighting. Keep the mortals chatting. Keep the Gods panting. Keep painting. Keep living. Keep creating. Keep building. Keep it going. Keep it moving. Keep it flowing. Keep in proving. Keep it showing. Keep on loving. Keep on growing. Never keep on slowing. Keep the kisses blowing. Keep the emotions flowing. Keep the stars glowing. Keep making love. Keep looking above. Keep singing with the doves. Keep holding her like a well fitted leather glove. Keep on keeping on.

Zeus Zooms

As the clouds part, in zero hours

Zeus will zestfully zap it into the ozone

With zox and zooks, we zeer down the trains, planes and zeppelin's

the zoologist studies the zounds that the zygotes make in zero Gs with the zephyrs

The zebra and zodiacs zealous zeer at Zambians

Close the zip-lock to the zealots zeal and zolt the zillions of zombies, as they zig zag and die slowly in zoodles of noddles

Zero in on the zenith and zipper down the zucchini

And find zen

Consider

Consider
All you know, you don't know
All you have learned is a dream state
And yet experience envelopes both dreams and reality

Conceived
By the light of nature by the grand creator of perfect existence
And yet experienced in all the imperfect and perfect states

Consider
The attrition that plagues this reality by the 6 senses
Deceiving the 6 senses with our very own 6 senses

Can I?

Can I move on with this? Can I move on from this? Can I move away from this? Can I move from left to right in this? Can I move 3 steps past this?

Can I move mountains ? Can I play in fountains? Can I count on this? Can I believe in this?

Can I question this? Can I sift through this? Can I move through this? Can I move along in spite of this?

Can I prolong this? Can I forego this? Can I predict this? Can I protect this? Can I be protected by this? Can I proclaim this? Can I imagine this? Can I forget this? Can I mistake all of this? Can I make mistakes in this? Can I still picture this? Can I miss this? Can I move back to this? Can I crash land into this?

Can I?

The China Set

Among the clay pottery, hand crafted

Hidden behind the hues of reddish brown, shaped and pattered earthen materials

Placed with matching little cups, mugs, vases and bowls

Decorated and shown

Hides the one china tea set

Embroider and polished in flowers of rose, lotus, lilies and bonsai

Water schemes flow on the shelf, encased with pristine ivory, filled with blues, yellows, and greens

The essence of Zen in many a garden

The presence of the creators hardship and handiwork for all to enjoy in the traditional tea ceremony

Created for the people, in the many facets of the beauty from the highest ingenuity and invention

Sit and drink

Passing

In the midst of the exiting warm summer weather

The people move about, the exhaust pipes from the cars, scream and shout
The gears move within the engines
The leaves dance about the shells of the cars
Among the suns warmth that we have never any doubt in

(With every passing change of the wind)
It all seems like
(Every passing hand on the clock)
Time and seasons pass onto the next rotation, cyclic and circular
Always onto the next passing

5 years

It was 5 years ago

to the year, to the month, to the day, to the hour, to the minute, to the second, to the split second

for the moment, for the sensation, for the emotion, into the expanse of the multi-verse

every 5 years, by the year, by the month, by the day, by the hour, the the minute, by the second, by the split second, on the clock, hand by hand, coo- coo by roster crow, sounding into the expanse of quantum physics

Past and present combine every 5 years

from the year, form the month, form the day, form the hour, from the minute, form the second, from the split second, leaving the moment, leaving the sensations, leavening the emotion dragging the multi-verse.

figuring that quantum physics and time

have a response of 5 years of happening

Paradoxically Prone

A creature of peculiar habits

a lagoon of eccentric algae

a mummy with adventurous talents

a joke with depressive qualities

a forum dressed and laughing like a clown encompassed in the outer abyss of inner dimensions

a folded equator

a line with no ending or mobius stripe

a dog without a scent

a millionaire who spends his money on helpful charities

in a circle, hangs a square triangle, balancing on the corner of an arc, looking at an elephant, tickling a mouse's toes

as a cricket plays Beethoven's 5th symphony, accompanied by a giraffe dancing to the busy bee, laughing with a kangaroo

as we humans learn all from history and glass shatters in the frozen air

a mirror filtered, a cellphone tells the truth, a calculator spells it out, when a pencil can erase the clouds from the rivers

as the fountain pen dries up

until the leper's sleep with the lions

until the prophet stammers on his foolish wisdom

when gravity pulls us forward, as inertia pushes us back

to the lessons learned by the lemurs and lapping leopards

at the end of the rainbow, the nymph eats the golden apple, cause

there is too many silver ducats frolicking in the opium fields

there is too much sense, to be showing skin and serenity to the shamans singing

One from the Heart

A fable with music
A distance between imagination and execution
One through the heart
Which leaves one to wonder
Why is the dream so much sweeter then the taste?
Music coffee makers
Gruff voice romanticizer
Its devilish, its an idea
Its on the nickel
One from the street corner
A distance close to imagination and realty
A beautiful ghost, a baffling host, in the most highest of junkyard
dogs
Why is the coffee so much more bitter then the smell?
Its one from the heart
A Las Vegas hooker finds herself in the streets of New Orleans
Que the orchestra, light another cigarette
And move with the fable of music
One from the heart

Rants

Robots recover the research and rewire the realms of reality

Rasputin recruits and razes the rightly roused red handed rants for rigorous reasons

Listen to the robins and ravens recite the rhymes

Revisions revive the requiem of the rose

Receive the reward

Reboot, realize, release, relish, repeat, repeat, repeat, repeat

Then rise

Revitalize the red readings of retrograde regression

Then reply in rants that resign the reason to the rainbows and repartee

Recline in the reckoning and roam in and out of the rhythm of repetitive revisions

What if?

A sphinx without a secret
A picture without a frame
A pyramid with no peak
A murder without blame
A cornerstone that is weak
A bubble with a leak
Days come after week
Speak it but also keep it

The many, before us

During the day
I moved around the yard enjoying my daily chores
When the sun is highest
I moved around the yard in my daily encounters with nature
Weed whacking, mowing the lawn and gardening
Among those times, through out the day
My mind did wander and wonder to and fro and from here to there
In the midst of that can be labeled Insanity
There arose a aura of brilliance rising from the earth
Faces of beauty
Moved with the wind
As I gazed on, I felt a peace with nature
A oneness with the many

Who are these many?
Who are these faces of beauty?

Surrounded by the beauty
In this moment, I realized the faces, the auras from the earth are
The ancestors, The archetypes, The ones that came before us
Our Teachers, Our shamans, The Gypsies, The Witches , The Wizards that harnessed the essence of nature

They are the ones who have become a part of the ethereal dance

The dance that will bestow all its secrets and sensuality on us, as we moved into the path that all kings and all queens have ventured before us

They now sit on the right hand of the grand creator

Lapping in luxury

Swaddled in the eternal peace

In those moments, in that beauty

As they dance in the ethereal

I dance with them in the human landscapes

Their presence, my presence

Moving together in wandering through my daily chores

Understanding that in the wondering of here and now and to and fro

Physical nature and the ethereal dance are linked and moving as one

We will be the many

We will be the faces of beauty

As Learn and listen to the many before us

Our Teachers and Shamans

The essence of nature and the grand creator

Before

Befriend the fall of the branches that betrayed the bombing in the
beautiful and bountiful
Beauty befalls the beast, before bells and the beast respond to
loves
beckoning
Before the break of bedlam, the bouncing Betty will blow the build-
ing far below the better believe in brains and blue eyes that are
brilliant, bodacious and blistering to the bombs bouldering blast
That's when the bastards while balance the bottle of backwater
ballads and basic breastfeeding
The bewilderment will brave the blasphemy and backsliding into the
basin of blemishes
Before hand, before man, before the band
The barometric bartenders will believe that the beaches and battle-
fields are full of brilliant bodies of beetles and birds
Balanced between 2 building the beatniks and bouncer bellow for
Beetle juice, beetle juice, beetles bopping in the broad-castings of
the blues
Bon Voyage

Stop Moving

Stop Moving
Look, listen, lustre
When the screams surround you
When rest eluded you
Stop moving
Look, listen, be still

A desire is upon you
Be still and know I Am Here
Be still and give no mercy to your fear
A desire, a reckoning to stop moving
Look, Listen, Be still and Know I am Here

The earth will shake
The mountains with tremble
The sea will split
The skies will crumble
As I walk, As I surround, As I hold you
Stop moving
Look, Listen, Lustre
For the whispers that follow the chaos
Stop moving
For I am the Calm
Look, Listen, Be still and Know I am Here

Inside

Inside the minds, is matter

Inside the matter, lives a molecule

Inside the molecule, is metaphysics

Inside metaphysics in the mind, the matter, the molecule with
metaphysics

So meditate on the moment

don't become locked inside like a manic in a rats maze

But mediate with movements in the minds matter and metaphysics

Pandemics and Discussion

Pandemics and Paintings
Discussions of Disasters
Paramedics and Pastors
Deliver duties
Pictures of Purpose
Dismal and Dizzy
Pens and Pencils
Draw out dead lines
Persons and peoples prepare
Distractions in daylight
Picturesque platitudes

Enough Time

When you spend enough time, looking past your nose and beyond
your phone

You will find that is passing, that people are build with a twist

A twist in their spine, a crooked left index finger, a pigeon-ed toed

split, a skip, a hop and jump in the crooked direction

Look long enough into the looking glass and you will see that
people all carry a lazy eye, in which we see all things possible

We are all mad here

Possibility is positiveness

Persuasion is from deformity

Perfection died before it was ever born, a long, long time ago

With the crooked sailor, the unknown solider, the bastard child, the
drowning rain dogs, the vagabonds that we all choose not to look at

That we all choose not to admit we all are

Walk long enough through the soil and all will find the growth of
beauty, of passion, of such brilliant people

We are all filled with scars, crooked fingers and many beautiful

deformities

live long enough and help each other move forward and stop sliding
backwards by embracing the broken, crooked, fragile, vertebra we
are all stumbling around in

Sane madness

Through the black hole
The preverbal rabbit hole
Where past, present and future are post humorous
We cant be late
For everyday is a very merry un-birthday to you
The roses are painted white
The cheschire cat in stripes
The table is set for the walrus and the carpenter
Oysters for all
Mustard and tea
For the best date
The clock strikes non
The dream is all undone
Reality comes rushing back in
And we are late
But all is such fun

Forget thy self

The greatest act of anarchism was when

She put the flower in the barrel of the gun

Or was it when

The Buddhist lite himself on fire showing that the oppression will
burn and all come undone?

All this happens for a demonstration of what happens when we

upset the status quo

And stop thinking about oneself

When a whisper makes all the difference

When a gesture of penitence is in show

In the bright and early suns glow

When you feel like you've reached the ultimate low that when it all
comes crashing down planned and slow

By a hand, a mind, by a human that was willing to let go of the ego
and move and be the example that finds the peaceful flow

That is when the greatest acts of humanity are driven outward,
onward into the bright, hopeful, better, more powerful future for the
masses to reflect on

The greatest act of activism is when you can forget thyself and
raise our hands together and help in the healing

Abstract alchemy

There stands the alchemist in an attire of atonement

the answers are so ambitious and alluring to the academics as they

have tried to apprehend the abandoned abatement in the abstract
arrays of atmospheres

With the appetite of alligators and angels attraction such attention

We can absorb the antiquated alabaster and align the acceptable

aspirations and apply them to the attrition that is appealing to the
albatross in the atom and only pull out aces on high to account for
the atomic ages alarm to the abstract of activity in the abyss

Learn

The surrealism sets in once in awhile when reading history and watching as we repeat it

Fully locked in a quarantine as a pandemic lurches outside our front doors

Black, Spanish, Red, Virus, Infect and Plague this world in the cycle like a carnival

Rolling through town, BIg top, clowns, Showing sights un scene for decades

What do we learn from such freak shows?

The Rhyme of Nature

A tree, a Plant, A shrub, a Hedge
A vow, A prayer,A thought, A pledge
A place, A palace, A face, a little Callous
A brick, A river, A lick, A cone
A lamp, A light, A champ, A sight
We sing, We dance, They sting, They lance
A player, A sailor, A whaler, A tailor
A mat, A hat, A bat, A cat
A cloud, A shroud, A haze, A maze
A poet will show it, The crowd will know it
A rhyme will tickle
A burger, A pickle
Politician are fickle
A leaky drain with trickle
In the dark, in the light
\in the day, in the night,
the pain, the pleasure
The free, the fettered
The before, the after
A page, a chapter
The sun, the moon
The dove, the loon
The silent, the sound
The smile, the frown
The stop, the go
To suck, to blow

Be Human

My Child. My Child
Don't stop your toil, don't let your crops go to spoil
Yes, the end is nigh but hold in your sad sigh
For we shall all die but hold off the pity till the end
Strive for passion till we find the light at the end of the prisms bend

My Love. My Love
Life is love and Love is pain
But without these blisters and blood stains
There is no victory or gained
So stand beside me, kiss my cheek
With your hands keep my heart, a beat
For the end is nigh but that is never a final goodbye

My Son. My Son
Write this down. Tie this up
And keep your memory smart
Don't let your heartstrings fall apart
They will break your heart. From first to last.
This heartache will pass
Like tears on your cheek, As blood running through the streets
And keep close to you, the eternal peace
Keep your hands raised and praise the holy above

My Daughter. My Daughter
Be mindful of all that is taught here
Mother Earth and Father Time
Have spread their hands in Loves chime, here
Don't forget, The Earth spins in and out
We are Humans, born to walk in Truth and Love
So don't let that fire inside fade out

My Children. My Children
Be kind to one another
Don't be another brick in the wall
Don't let love fall, behind the cover
But answer that triumphant call
Be here, be near, Be Human
For as Peaceful people, we shall never fall

Be Human. Be Human

Windows

We view out the windows and view the willows, waving to the wid-
ows
Who are stuck in wandering in the ways of the wise
Whispers to the wind
We begin walking and waking, as we wait for the weeping at the
wishing well
As the wasps whiz through the wisdom of wounds and wade in the
wreckage of wrath
We weigh what the wise will wish when wonderland is the waste-
land
We waste not, what we wanton not
And without tomorrow
We are without yesterday
We also whistle and today and the west wing
The wayward wonder-kin use watercolour to weave the weeks and
witness the winos trying to use weapons
Wipe away the who's, the why's, the what's and when's for the wiz-
ards and witches
And now we must wake up and write about the wishing wells win-
dows
Wearing white wardrobes and waistcoats

Is It

Is it?

The beauty in the mundane?

Or is it

The beauty of the insane?

Will it all matter, once we meet the true maker?

The burning factor or the blessed soul taker?

In a cyclic existence with no intrinsic awareness to be broken and in
darkness, we stumble around with a passive carelessness

Light blind in dark minds

But as the lotus grows through the mire

We can all reach the halo on the highest spire

We may have to cross the lines, blur the design, and erase the

egos chime

To reach the beautiful transcendent human kind

But we shall be the light bending through the cracked pyre

So is it

The beauty in the sun that's over and done?

Or is it

The beauty in the moon that will be well hung?

So is it

The beauty in the morning song?

Or is it

The beauty in the night forever hung?

The News

We watch the news to feed our fears
To vicariously stroke the electric fuzz of our egos
(this wont happen to me)
Yet the News only proves we are helpless
Yet still petting our egos to find out, that maybe we are something
more then few

Careless and unattainable

The news shows were nothing more then dying cells, deteriorating
into something left for worst

Strange signs

Speak to the sutra of the shamans spiritual sermon

Sneak to the shores of the strange

Silently see Solomon slip into the songs of such scenery and sounds of the slightest skip, which will sear into the smooth skin of silk and satin

Speak to strangers because strangers are never strangers, their just servants in second sight

Speak what is spoken

The sublime is scarring the sky

The sea is swimming in the stars

Remember that Satan and Simon started sinking into the sea after they severed as slaves to selfishness

Stand in the shine of the star gazers

Sound the singles of the shoe gazers

Swirl the secrets in snow covers slopes

Schizophrenics sneeze and sleep in a state of syndication

As The sirens are singing to seduce the sailors and soldiers that are stumbling up the stairs, so they can sit on the stool to see you as soon as the sun shines on the scales of the snake

As it slithers and shimmers through the sands of the Sahara and- shows the systems of skirting the sinister sisters soviet satire

Serenade the sea shells on the sea shore to see sally sail into Salisbury hill

filled stealth and short strains of smoke

I miss writing with pen on paper

I miss writing on paper!!

Feeling my hand smudge the ink of the chicken scratch I call odes, sonnets and poetry

Feeling the palms sweaty and strained well holding the tool that is mightier then the sword

Feeling the power of ideas flowing in a liquid that has stained societies for centuries

Feeling the release of pressure, insecurities and travel logs for all to read

This could be a dream!!

But the paper in front of me is soaked in steam....all the friction from flesh on flesh. Skin on skin, stitched together by the strands of thin inked lines we lay all around in fictions inspiration

Friction from paper and pen, paragraph and story, words and sentences, letters and forms... Period

I miss writing with pen!!

Sitting, alone with thoughts waiting for the fingers to receive the twitch from the heart strings to start a singing

To receive the unbelief or belief to deceive and have fiction reign supreme

Scratches and swirls. Mistakes and edits. Re-edits. Re-edits. Re-edits. A Coffee break. Never to let the pen touch the table in a horizontal way. More Re-edits. A cigarette break

I miss writing on paper with pen

A signature feels more Ernest when there a swift flash from the pen

Coffee House

Coffee house rituals. Milk. Cream or sugar spindles
Stir pretentiously
Sip and glance around to view all the other hipsters, poets, intel-
lects and humans
Drinking their sauce of inspiration and perceptions balance.
As brain waves connect conceptions pure depictions.
Speak in sips, Morse code of souls
Holes in soles
Its always raining. We always speak of pain.
Yet
All is fair in Love and War.
Rituals, riots, rants, reborn.
 For a blissful existence of peace.
Forget all who have scorned and just believe in the reborn.
In the coffee house, boundaries are broken. Vegan, carnivores,
transgender-ed, homo sapience
All these labels are a bore!!
Love. Love of coffee. Love with no end is.....
What we are all hoping for
Love with no end.....
Will happen in these coffee houses

Visions

In visceral vermilion, the 7 virgins view vainglorious of valour

Vent the voiceless with videos and viciously visualize the vivid vase,

as it disappears into vapors and the villains start venturing venge-
fully through Virginia

The veil of Maya covers the valley

And ventilates the very vagueness

As ships and sails voyage through the well which holds onto the
visions veins

Virtues are viewed and vices are vivisected into vomit

Vindicate those vows that visit voting booths of the vernacular

Release the vulgar vultures to veer into vines of variables and vari-
eties in the company of vagabonds and vagrants

Vicariously view the void

Muse. Lover.

more than a muse
Much more in a lover
No artistic abuse. A safe place to hide in her glorious cover
Stand with me. Stand with me.
Helping each other be all we can be
Oxoxxoxo
I'm your Zeus. You my Aphrodite
In a hive of buzzing bees. Be my sweet honey
Those calm waves in this turmoil-ed sea
This is the end. Which my love, we will never see
Its just you and me. The world will bow to thee
They will see. All I see. In those bright blue eyes
For futures alive and clean
Gleam forward. Glisten towards all life's beauty
My Heavenly Demon, my everything. Such a cutie

more then a muse. Much more in a lover
Stay beside me. Be my protective cover.
The shelter from this dismal scene
Close my eyes, release the refreshing concept of love in you and
me
From heaven this has been a genius of much more then hellish sin
Sprawled out. Laying. Intertwined. Layer upon layer
Of
Satisfied. Satisfied. Satisfied. Orgasms into ecstasy.
In and out of penetrating reality

Souls reached. Souls touched. Souls longing for more then a muse. Much
More then a lover
Passion. Ecstasy. Satisfied with a humans sexual expression
More then a muse. Much more in a Lover

Gather

Go, go gadget go
Governments govern like good gods yet gamble and lead with
greed and death, like the grim reaper, reaping gourds and grapes
Gnomes gyro in the grounds with gallant groups of Gypsies gather
together with grace
Greet the giants om greener grass
And wave goodbye to the groups of gun that gore with gross gan-
der of gossip
Wave hello to girlfriends and gaze into the great kiss in the gardens
of grace and gorgeous gestures
don't fall into gloomy glimpses of grave gatherings
Watch the geese and grasshoppers graze
And guard the guitars guides into the gyroscope

King of sunder, Queen of Kool

We swore that 2 lives shall be as 1
For as along as the seagull loves the sea and the sunflower sought
the sun
My love will pass on from me to you
For I am the King of sunder and you are the Queen of Kool

Locked and loaded in bright blazing blue eyes
My love There is nothing we should rue
For you are the beauty and I am the art
And for that neither one of us shall be apart
We shall watch our love fly
As we pour on the gasoline, we will light up the skies and burn this
town to smithereens
let the ivory palace turn into ashes to ashes
And like a phoniex rising from the ashes
Our will ascend with the sun beams
For I am the king of sunder and you are the Queen of Kool

Locked and loaded in bright, blazing blue eyes
Shall we lay down in a bed covered in rose pedals, revitalized and
awoken
While the nightingales blister the skies, they can not sing a note or
pierce their breast to show how much our love will provide
For there is nothing we shall rue
For I am the King of sunder and you are the Queen of Kool

Light up my fire, burn like the funeral pyre and lets show this world
how to die like Romeo and Juliet'

Held together in the 7th delight of heaven

Fore I love you, my little flutter by
Beauty in the sight of mine eye
I love you, little lily
Flower into my existence so I can forget my pity
I Love you, My queen of Kool
My cleanse pool, my Capernaum healing pool
Swing into Love, as you lay above
And strange as it is speak to me of the gardens you have tended
too
For Roses are red, Violets are Blue, you are pristine in sight and I
love you
For I am the King of Sunder and you are the Queen of Kool

Keep keeping

On safari the kangaroos kick and keep keys in keep and kept the secrets of kale and knives

Keep knitting and killing while we kiss in the kitchen and try to kid the kaleidoscopic

Kids and kittens kidnap the kidney stones and kiwis for the koala bears to find the keystones and key points

Nurture Abundance

Vibrate
With the sun
Pulsate
With he moon
Run
With the wind
Swim
With eh water
Live by the influence of nature
Nurture the effects of the peaceful and powerful deities
Moving as one, becoming as one
Tethered by one, play from the harp that crescendo from the outer realm
That surrounds us
With music, laughter and abundance

Time and Dates

Time
Is not linear
Dates
Can not be perceived by here or there
Time
Falls all around us
Dates
Scatter like dust
Time
Has happened already
Dates
It happened already

Reverb

Unbridled noise
The shrieking on the horizon
Thurston Moore
Sputtering and Stretching strings
It draws you in on the repulsing of the amps
Waves of feedback, turning in and out of the air
Words splattering among the onlookers
In a violent, yet untheartening way

Coffee house pt. II

Drink coffee. View through a window. Breath oxygen. Feel the blowing wind. Prick thy finger. Pluck thy thorn from thy side. Coffee stains. Stressed brains. Vanities veins. Stomachs twists and turns. Conscience yearns and burns. Celestial bodies in burn. As earthly bodies year after years turn. Twilight zones. Hungers bone. Words cant cast stones. A loud conversation on a private phone. My love. Push me down on a bed of foam. Kiss me. I feel alone. Sitting drinking coffee, sugar. Sweet as thy kiss. Stoic. Captured in stone. A light from above. Easter island. Druids of England. Celtic rants. Shamans chants. With coffee there's no "cants" . Drink coffee observe all these tales and legends. Through pages and pages of Generations and generations of centuries and eons history .

Wrath eating

History is full of philosophy

In as much as we are filled with molecules that perceive life's beginnings

History is not fully written by the victors

The ones who lost and where hanged, prison-ed, crucified and exiled wrote the master class of history

Bringing pages and pages to their accusers in order for a message to be revealed

Tongues opened to the brains synopsis

Opened to each-other to realize that to reform reality we must replace nothing

Let the light of nature

The birth of tragedy

The symposium Leviathan

Swim into the void-less abyss

Circling and surfing all words and knowledge

Are we all searching for the utopia

That has come and went?

or are we all just walking backwards into oblivion as we have started wrath eating ourselves because we don't like how history has played out?

Fun and fancy free

The feeling of fear is frightening and frozen in footsteps forever in fear and fore longed the frenzy of frantic facts and features

Frost and foreshadowing is Forever the 4th frontier which will fracture from the first frost on the foreground

Forgive the first fragile form of the forgotten 4 horsemen

And the frown

It was framed by a foreign friend and foe who fought the 5th frenzy of freedom and fun and fancy free

We can call be fun and fancy free in field of flowers, frolicking with the foxes and flutter bys

And that is the framework to a friendly fight in fields of familiar yet foreign firearms and fingers

While the figures of family and foes touch the faces o=
for the forehand and for mentioned fun and fancy free

Idle Freedom

In the late early hours
We peel back the notion of freedom
Which sets fourth
Anxiety,which is the dizziness of freedom
A desire feeding the unneeded

That as leisure creates idle hands
It will lead to mischief and blossom into murderdom
Thrown into a open chasm
Narrow your heart to discipline
Quench, your mind to few options
Reserve, your habits to spiritualized actions
One by one

The Grimy Deep

Speak to me of the angels and the sea
Of how many hearts from them came to be
Broken, Lost, Profound and with what cost?
Did they search for the need to be lost?

A stammering and stutter
A choice of waves and tides
Of silk hair and drowning affair
Did they all have to fight against the shore and thunder?

Speak to me of captain and sailors
Of the menacing death dealers
That course through the grimy deep
To roam all they could not see
From sea to shinning sea

Its the stammering and stuttering
In the white curls of the deep
Its in the pursuing and forging for these treasures that tried to keep
By sword, by pistol, by plank, by crystal
After the storms the boats did creep
As the water seeps and all the men venture to the grimy deep

Jugglers

We have joined the jagged jaguars jogging's
We have joined the jolts of the jeeps journey
We have jailed the jigsaw killer in his jaundice
We have found juries jabbing in juxtapositions the juices
There are judicial jackals jetting and judging in juvenile justice
We have jumped into Jupiter junkies
We have jammed , jam and jelly into the jargon of jeopardy
As we jingle and juggle with jitters and jokes filled with javelins
We jog on into jet streams and find joyful, joy rides
As we play jump rope with the jugglers

Death

and in Death, we do not die. We strike a match, We dance with I. The blameless and Free

We find the original mind when darkness has been lifted, We become a new kind.

with belts and burlap we shed and say goodbye

with wings and halos we adorn, we sail into the sky

For angels we are, and angels we become out of the ordinary, out of the slums, ascending to heaven, no longer picking up crumbs

for now, in death, we eat at the decorated table

We let our minds embrace as one and become stable

the brilliant, the beauty, the furrows, the fable

and we realized we are prudent and capable

to be reached and received

For the first become last and the last become first

So eat and be merry, we have seen all life's glory

In the Death, our bodies become warm, light floating, ascending, meditating on a plain, A higher dimension.

that during our birth we could now mention

although we have watched the sunflower wilt

the rose fade and the diamond smudge

we have lifted those visions and stared into the sun

find that the sunflower, the rose, the diamond have moved onto a place that is never ending

a place that never finds our purpose to be over and done

In Death, we are born again
shielding what was left and leaving all that is mortally done
A personally journey, my daughters, my sons
Be at Peace, Find Harmony
but lift your eyes to the Death we all become

Lights

Light the lamp that is lingering in lessons of love
Listen, lose your lustre and list the lusts
The lion will lay with the lamb
Lullabies will lull the leopards
So we can lick liquorice and find leeches and lichens on the lightning
The lethargic lepers lure the lost leprechauns and show the lords and lexicons how to laugh at lollipops and rainbows
Lounge long and lasers will last longer
Latitudes and longitudes are lay lines, that lead to the labyrinth that lead belly lingers in
Its all lifestyles and loops that leap in light years

A kiss

You were something so different, in a place so familiar
I've seen the lotus bloom through the grimy deep
and the rose explode into water

I've viewed the blue crested, red breasted finch, buzz by the
hummingbirds nectar
in those moments. I can't recall if I ever kissed you on your neck before?

In the kitchen, there's a cat in a box
but it is not Schrodinger's Cat, she's more like the Cat in the Hat looking
for this and for that
the music sounds off the morning
with the Kool breeze want of the evening
In those moments, I can't recall if I have ever kissed your hand before

It all seems like a close encounter with a dying spectre
As a small speck of light is sequestered
in the box where the Cat and the Hat, look for this and for that
and falls into the Grimy deep
we find the petals of rose coloured water
which proves that metaphysics can only be sensible in ostracized
situations
where there is something so familiar
in a place that seems so different

and in those moments, that is where I kissed your forehead

I held your hand

and we moved through dimensions and became 2 bright specters sipping
the hummingbirds nectar

Use the usual

The use of the unusual uttering of understanding will ultimately undress the useless undertone of utility

UFOs have the utensils to move upward and find Ulysses unable to unite the urchins unchanging umbrella

Its all ultra ubiquitous to ask the unquestionable, the uncommon undertow in this unlimited universe

Untie the under takers underworld

The Rest

To wander

As a dying breed

To wonder

In this dying meed

Saunter on a mighty steed, with mind and tongue of such speed

To speak the truth and have The Rest spit on the prove, hot coals of a
dying fire

They started burning books, lighting their own funeral pyre

They burned a witch for see healed the sick

They dying breed will sit in the balance, silent and laughing at all The Rest

As they feast on all the chemicals and T.V. captions

The Rest never stop talking for fear that they might be found out how
short they fall

Or they might actual hear the truth, that they didn't know

If the tongue never ceases moving

Then it will be come fragile, and be found in wanting

With its host living in disillusion

Hello

HI, Hello, How are you?

Shout hosanna in the highest, so that all the half breeds and hail Mary's heed your happiness

Hence fourth, heroism, hedonism….also heroin leaves behind half baked hallways circling in hallucinating hearts and hair pieces

Hover over the hollies that scale the hallows and hallways of heaping hills, that are haunted by the headless horse men

In heavens , in havens, in hoping in the heavy hours

The hives of hundreds and hundreds live in havoc

Hares inhabit houses and help with husbandry and hoarding honey

Hide the helping hands and heed the howling of hounds at the hung hangings

Why has all this happened?

Why are humans still unhappy and healing?

The Rose

In the deepest, darkest, dreary recess of the human mind
Stands
A rose, in purest form of your lovers abstract
Waiting to be kissed

The Rose
Is the power of the warm touch of your lover under the kool veil of silk
sheets
Hidden beyond the thorns lies beauty not yet comprehended by the human
abstract

Picturesque

Take in the mosaic of the legends, in all its kaleidoscope of spinning scenes

(picturesque forums)

The aroma of seasons

The breath of functioning reasons

There flowing, cascading, through the cavalcade of emotions

Creating a Mosaic of (picturesque prepossession)

Come here, my love, kiss me, show passers by how picturesque the dirty streets are

Slither sideways down the sidewalk to show how spectacular and picturesque the entity and present moment can be

Drink up (the picturesque essence)

Reveal (the picturesque Acquiescence)

Yield to (the picturesque request)

Of mellow yellow, as it flows, as it cascades through the cavalcade of (the picturesque Perceptions)

Move in the mosaic of bricks (a picturesque Landscape)

Flowing waters onto (a picturesque Japanese Tea ceremony)

Blossoming lotus, an explosion (of picturesque moments) from the grimy

deep

Its picturesque in the morning, its picturesque in the afternoon, its picturesque in the evening

(remember the scene) for its all picturesque

(radiant at best, Hidden)

In picturesque forums

Linger on the mosaic of flavors

Dancing on the tongue in (a picturesque foxtrot)

Flowing, cascading with the cavalcade (of picturesque spices) onto a palate (of picturesque pleasures) tiptoeing onto innocent nerves

Sitting around the table (with picturesque plates) prepared to forum a mosaic (of picturesque tastes and sense)

(Enjoy her) picturesque positions

(Relishes his) picturesque prose's

(romanticize a) mosaic of interlocking, intertwined (picturesque limbs)

The mosaic (of picturesque flesh and passions)

All flowing, cascading to enhance the cavalcade of (every picturesque moment) in this picturesque Life

Move

The manic must ask you a mistake of menacing, masked mysteries of

meaning

Under the memoirs of the mustache

Move over so the meek will migrate to the mused missions of the millions
and millions of multitudes of marching marsupials

Meet the minds and make amends

Learning music must move in the mist and misunderstanding

To make sure we do not misstep on mars or mercury

We must find the models of the mill stone and mile stones in the mundane

March with more morals because mortals can have malice to the
microwaves of the mini mice

The mandate is more meticulous and metric

For Morphous moves in the matrix that made the music motionless in

matter

Morphous moved in mountains and moving myths as the mirrors thought
millenniums are misguiding to memories

Martyrs found no mercy

As a murder of crows manoeuvre on the movies mishaps in media and
mouthed that there is a mouthful of marbles

So the moose mumbled some mournful motives

Whisper

IN the moon light, I always hated how you can look through my head

So stand still thy great knight and let the errors of your ways cease into the
atmosphere of time

stop this heart, with that I will pay, start through the night and enjoy through
all tomorrows days

as we watch the closets blues be created in the closest heavens

she had satin lips, hypnotizing hips, and man when were kissed……what a
glorious splendid trip

Have me linger of your finger tips, let me dance on the lips of your tulips and
run naked across the open horizon

Catching the scent of the early morning

let me words drip on your sweet red lips

as we dance on the out sand of time, and leave our footprints embedded in
the sands of time

as we whisper, whisper, whisper these sweet stinging prose's

Let us become lost, as we make my bed, as we make your bed, as we make
this place a lovely homestead

and praise the flesh, the beauty of nature

a scent so fresh, as we cuddle into nurture

step into the this wild, wild behaviour

and whisper, whisper, whisper these sweet stinging prose's

Now will that be enough to satisfy the thirstiest of men?
don't be careless with ones souls
for we will have 100 hands held together as we show that Love is the tether
that will hold this world together
and we will make this tether shine better and brighter then Gods smile
now will that be enough to satisfy the thirstiest of men?

So stand still thy great prince and let the errors of your ways seep into the
depths of the shadows and caves
and whisper, whisper, whisper these sweet stinging prose

in the moon l light, you always hated How I could look through your head

Troubles of today

Terra forum the terrace as time tickles the transformer and touches the turtles toes into tap dancing

Trick or treat?

That's the tough of it all

That's the tear in the tether

Tattoos tell tantalizing tales of triumph in tonal tones

Tripping on the twinkle in time

Tackle the wrinkle in time

Talk with the tactless texture and take the tincture that will turn today into tonight then into tomorrow and thirty times together

There's 200 tongues tied to the tangos that are twitching and twisting

travail through the tulips the tightly try to tire out tonight's thankless typecast teaching in 2 dozen trees

tilt the tile

Tease the troll

Trigger the turmoil of the tectonic technology

When trouble rolls in like tumbleweeds

The Trance in tenderness and thundering in thoughts

Thinking entity

To study, to search, to seek, to breath, to paint, to write, to play, to dance, to speak

To comprehend, to understand, to conceive, to contemplate, to think, to adore, to visualize, to vocalize, to conceptualize

Is to philosophize in all the manners that have been deemed to man, A thinking entity

The entity to think for thyself and play as a child in the sand box of knowledge

In which we love and love well

To dig deeper, more profoundly into understand

Which will lead us onto more thinking and digging

The deeper we go, the more we still need to know

Grasping

In the grasping of knowledge, I have realized, there is nothing to
grasp for

The pursuit of knowledge is like standing at a precipice of a cliff on
the edge of a black hole

Then as you pace on that razors edge, you slip on a banana peel,

spill your coffee on your white shirt and begin to fall,

as you try to grasp at a passing star or rock formation

You realize, there is nothing to grasp for

And start to embrace the fall you have slip into

The grasping of knowledge comes from learning it has been a part
of you in the journey

You just had to sit down and sip you coffee

Human nature

To give birth
And
To give into death
Those are the most intrinsic human behaviors
They begin, as they end
Everything in the middle is of a different nature
Esoteric to the most intelligent minds

Ideas

Ink the inside of the ideas, the ideals, no the ideas
And try To identify the inner insects of inter section in ions
Do not ignore the insane to find the ideology on the intrinsic import-
ant invention
I is I
It is ice cold with the interest of immature imaginations
To ignite the infusion of inter-stellar idleness and the infection of the
inner iris
In all respect, in all manner of speaking, inaction is inches away
from the important interstate of insidious industries
Identify the insecurities and inquest of the injustice to the incumbent
inconsistencies of infinity
I and I is Not I and I
Inside the incisions is the inviting inconclusive encounter of
I and I

Love With No End

My father sat me on his knee under the big oak tree
And begin to speak of life. He said " son, people will hate you for the
love you have for them"
So
Walk this world in a straight and narrow path. And when you are look-
ing back on all you have traveled you can say
There is nothing to hide and my soul is full of rightious pride

He told me of the times he spend watching people die for a country
That would hide their bodies. Lost in the grime and crime of war
Yet we still find this country is worth fighting for

As we sat under the sun. He spoke of times to be undone.
He said regret nothing and be a inspiration and muse for those who
do.
For they have not seen what they run from and find only emptiness
under the sun

As we walked the path that leads back home.
He looked down and spoke about LOVE
Telling me to find a woman. A woman as beautiful and cunning and
caring as your mother

And when you do son, make sure to show her, you love her more
then life its self and enjoy all that she has brought to your life. And
as you move through life together be glad for all the positive inspi-
ration. The beautiful depictions and the brilliant perception in ma-
neuvering though society and all its strife. Love her with all of life
But above all

LOVE HER WITH NO END

He also said "son, don't stop searching, seeking and smiling.

For walking down this street, lit by only a few street lamps.

Being surrounded by a crowd

But feeling like your shadow is the only one to understand.

And As you walk to the station.

Ending a run of such importance with elaborate meaning

The cynic in you speaks " this was a bloody waste"

But The optimist in you whispers "this is what you've longed for"

To the people who surrounded you. All you can say is " thank you
my friends"

Never to forget what you found out and learned

What truly lies in your soul

Remembering that after the thunder rolls. And the lighting cracks

The next morning is a sight of calm beauty. Like when you saw
yourself in the mirror for the first time

After she said "I love you"

The past is now flashed away

The present embrace by the here and now

And the future is watching in the distance.... remember to always
LOVE THIS WORLD WITH NO END